"I've known Wes Lyons for most very close and, while growing up, we both attended the same church. In a word, he's always been a person of high character. You can bet your bottom dollar that when it comes to Wes, he is going to do the right thing. He is a truly passionate person that will find success in any endeavor he chooses to pursue simply because he is destined for greatness!!"

Lousaka Polite, *Fullback, Atlanta Falcons*

"As a coach, you cross many paths with individuals, some that last a lifetime. Wes is one of those individuals, from day one, where there was that special connection that I knew would last a lifetime. Aside from being a gifted athlete and football player, Wes Lyons is an individual with impeccable character, work ethic, intelligence, and an inner drive to be the very best at whatever he does. Wes is and will always be considered a son to me. He is one of those individuals who have definitely impacted me and my family in a positive manner. I am very proud to say that I had the opportunity to coach Wes Lyons. He is mature beyond his years, and has a tremendous story that everyone should listen to."

Butch Jones, *Head Football Coach, University of Cincinnati*

"Wesley's journey in life epitomizes the virtues of patience and discipline. His focus and determined approach to the pursuit of his goals have encouraged both his contemporaries and elders. His undying faith is the core essence of who he is and all that he represents as a citizen of the world. He makes those connected to him very proud. His story is truly inspiring!"

Robert E. Young, *Pastor, New Hope Baptist Church*

"Wes being wise beyond his years understands it is through patience that the greatest goals are achieved to receive the most precious gifts."

Pat White, *Quarterback, Miami Dolphins,*
West Virginia University

"Wes preceded me at Woodland Hills High School where the "WH" stands more for "Work Hard." He is one of many division I football players from there and whose pursuit of success came through dedication and commitment. Wes embodies the "WH" mentality which led us both to the highest level of college football and the NFL."

Rob Gronkowski, *Tight end, New England Patriots*

"I always admire how hard Wes works on & off the field. I never got to play with him but would have loved having a teammate like him"

Quincy Wilson, *Assistant Director of Football Operations, West Virginia University*

"Throughout his entire football career Wes had to overcome many setbacks. He did it with hard work, perseverance and patience. Wes Lyons has spent about two decades of his life playing football. He's grown and developed into an outstanding young man. Wes is a man of high moral fiber and impeccable character. Many people have played a role in his development. Most important were his parents and family. They stood beside him in good times and bad. His many coaches and teachers from pee-wee football through high school, college, and the pro's all had an influence on his development. In his 20 year journey through football and life, Wes has gone through many obstacles and changes. He's handled himself amazingly in the pursuit of his dreams. Everyone that's been a part of his life has been extremely impressed with the young man that Wes Lyons has become. I'm sure anyone, especially past and present athlete's and football players, will enjoy hearing about Wes's many experiences in his Pursuit with Patience."

George Novak, *Head Football Coach, Woodland Hills*

"Having the honor of being a friend and business associate of Wes Lyons Sr., I had the pleasure of watching a child raised right grow into an outstanding young man. Wes Jr. is about perseverance, integrity and loyalty. This young man has me excited about the future! "

Chuck Sanders, *CEO, Urban Lending Solutions*

"Wes Lyons is a man with great core qualities: the core qualities of character, morals, values, and self-discipline. These qualities along with great faith are the cornerstone of making a difference in the life of others. Opportunities and success are only obtained by those special individuals that inspire change. Wes Lyons is one of those special people that will inspire change for many years to come. His book will inspire and motivate people from all walks of life. It is a must read."

Eugene Napoleon, *Author, CEO of Nap Records/Nap Sports*

"Wes has always been a great teammate, friend and mentor throughout the years. He is a wonderful person and an ideal role model for all student athletes. I congratulate him on all of the success that he has earned through persistence, hard work and dedication."

Will Johnson, *Fullback, Pittsburgh Steelers*

"I have known Wes Lyons for over 20 years. Our fathers were best friends and at an early age they instilled in us the values of hard work, perseverance, and making good decisions. Those values have provided opportunities on and off the playing field and, for that, I am very thankful. Just as our fathers instilled core values in us, I am sure that after reading this book the same values will be in you."

Ryan Mundy, *Safety, Pittsburgh Steelers*

"Wesley Lyons is a man of God, my best-friend, an inspiration for all young African American men, and a genuine leader. *"The Pursuit with Patience"* is a journey into a man's lifelong passion, both good and bad, that touches upon struggle and the human experience. Be patient, stay true, and follow your dreams; they can lead to places beyond imaginable."

Kirk L. Casey-Holloway, *United States Air Force*

"In a world that's all about 'me', Wesley Lyons is one of the few people I know who still cares about 'we'. He would never trade morals for success, or try to better himself at the expense of others. He's the type of person whom you don't have to tell a second time. If he says he's going to do it, consider it done. He goes wholeheartedly into everything that he pursues. His passion for what he does can only be outshined by his genuine care for others. He uses his influence as a role model to positively impact the youth. From playing professional football at the highest level; to every setback that he has encountered along the way, he has remained the same humble guy through and through."

Devon Lyons, *President of Beyond Phenom*

"Wesley I hope you know how proud I am of you. You have grown and are continuing to grow into a strong influential black man. You've finished college in 3 ½ years without any debt, you've had the opportunity to be a part of two NFL teams, and now this, an author of your own book. I'm loving it! I love watching you grow into who you are. I'm so proud and I love you."

Marva LaMar, *Mom*

This book is dedicated to my father. I'm very thankful for the commitment and impact he has made in my life.

THE

PURSUIT

WITH

The Pursuit with Patience

Copyright ©2012 by Wesley Lyons

wesleylyons.com

Ordering Information:
Special discounts are available on quantity purchases by corporations, associations, and others. For details, contact the publisher at the web address above.

Cover designed by Devon Lyons
Pictures purchased from US-presswire with permission

Contents

"Words mean more than what is set down on paper. It takes the human voice to infuse them with deeper meaning."
-Maya Angelou

Foreword

"The only way of finding limits of the possible is by going beyond them into the impossible."
-Arthur C. Clarke

In the career of a teacher, many students pass in and out of classroom but, if you are lucky, there are a few that you can see will be successful immediately. This is true for Wesley Lyons. As a student in the Woodland Hills High School, where football reigns supreme, Wes stood out as not only an athlete, but also a terrific young man. It soon became apparent that he was not just a good football player.

As he walked into my classroom, the first day, I was amazed at his height and his shy, quiet demeanor. He exhibited a strong desire to learn and soon became a class leader asking questions that encouraged his peers to engage in the various topics. His humor soon emerged and I knew that there was more to Wesley Lyons than one initially sees.

With the love and guidance of his family he was able to separate himself from many of his peers. While still a teenager, Wes had a vision for his future and he pursued that goal everyday with the same diligence as he did on the football field, while in High School, in College and the Pros. While disappointments have recently occurred, he continues to work towards that goal.

Wesley Lyons is a role model for athletes, young and old, but also for anyone that has a vision, the heart, and persistence to do the work.

Knowing his intensity, I am sure that everyone who reads this book will agree that Wesley Lyons is a very special young adult that will continue his "Pursuit with Patience."

Barbara Weiser

Introduction

In 2011, I started to write *"The Pursuit with Patience"* when I was released from the Pittsburgh Steelers. I originally thought about writing a book in 2010 when I first graduated from college, but I never thought I would because I hated to write. As time went on, and I was approached by the right people, I realized that it was possible as long as I put my mind to it. My intention, and what inspired me to write this book the most, was the opportunity to encourage the youth to read. I see so many young children who have very little passion about education. My goal of this book is to inspire at least one person. That would make all the hard work and time that I have dedicated to writing "The Pursuit with Patience" worth it in the end. I recall a time when I was playing for the Steelers and was approached by a 16 year old boy. He was a hoodlum, but he knew who I was and looked up to me. He said, "Wes, continue to ball....... Do it for all of us in the hood." These are the types of people that I have the power to affect and influence positively. I can not only influence young people by playing football, I can also help educate them with this book. I want to show them that athletes are capable of doing so much more than they received credit for. I took so much of my time and effort to make "The Pursuit with Patience" possible. I used to go to work/practice, then come home and spend countless hours writing this book. This was a great outlet for me to vent about the frustration that I was having. I was able to turn my frustration into something that would be positive and hopefully help others. There were quite a few times when I wanted to quit writing this book, but I realized that nothing was easy and I was determined to give it my all, like I did everything else. It took patience, consistency, and dedication to finish this book.

"The Pursuit with Patience" is not a book about the awards and success that I had in football; it's about the journey of my life. I really want people to understand the journey that I endured. At times fans may talk about you or praise about how good you are, but there's much more to being an athlete. This book breaks down just how genuine athletes are. I know and want to stress that all things are possible through God, who saved me. I am a young man who grew up in the slums of North Braddock, Pennsylvania and by believing and staying on the right path, I achieved amazing things.

Early Years in Sports

CHAPTER ONE

"Let no one despise you for your youth, but set the
believers an example in speech, in conduct, in love, in
faith, in purity"
-1Timothy 4:12

Before signing my first NFL contract with the Steelers;

before donning blue and gold in the hills of West Virginia;

even before my first days of school as a young boy in

Pittsburgh, there is one memory that I've held the longest—

running around a field at only three years old and swinging

feverishly during my first game of T-ball. Even though I

was playing only T-ball, I had a blast just running around

the field. The game introduced me to the world of baseball

and, more importantly, to the world of sports. I discovered a

realm of fun and competition. I was hooked. Whether I

was on the field or in the stands, from that moment, sports

held a special place in my heart. Little did I know, as an adventurous kid with a new-found passion, that the new surge of pride and burn of determination that I felt had officially laid the foundation for something children across the country dreamed of — life as a professional football player.

I must give credit where credit is due: my father, Wes Lyons Sr., was a MAJOR influence in my life, not only as a child, but also as an adult. Whether I trudged reluctantly to a practice when I'd rather be playing in the house, or wrestled with the discouragement of a team loss, my father was always there with a wise word and a true coach's perspective. Although I failed to realize it when I was younger, he was responsible for introducing me to being a "team player." Even as youngsters, he would encourage me and my brother, Devon, to do our very best. My father would coach us, motivate us and remind us that we could reach any goal that we set our minds to.

My older brother, Devon, has been a huge influence in my life as well. Devon is a couple years older than me, and when I was younger, I wanted to be just like him (whether it was good or bad). Devon's calm, caring demeanor and goofy side always provided me a sense of security. Even when he and I were getting into innocent mischief together and brainstorming airtight alibis that our father might believe, we were always a team. Devon did not realize it at the time, but he was such a great role model for me. The friendly competitions of an encouraging older brother with such self-discipline made me want to stretch a little further and go out of my "comfort zone." Even the simplest things like playing catch in our backyard, or just hanging out and playing any type of sport, strengthened our bond and influenced me greatly.

As I mentioned, my journey in sports began when I was only three years old. No matter what sport we were playing or how young we happened to be at the time, my father had a strong belief in training. While other kids were enjoying their leisure time after school and during the summer, my father was always keeping us busy with more training. We might have grumbled a bit, but we never complained to him (at least not too often).

By the age of eight, I really excelled in baseball. I played second base, short stop, occasionally pitched and even played in the outfield. I took part in the Diamond Skills tournament, which measured one's talents and abilities as a baseball player. My hitting, running and

fielding ability were reviewed, and I scored "off the charts!"
Not only did I make it into the national championship, but I
also hold the record for an eight-year-old in the Diamond
Skills to this day.

Imagine being that young, while people cheer you on
and tell you what a great ball player you are. And, even
better, I got to meet some great baseball players, including
Sammy Sosa and Mark McGwire. I think I was on cloud
nine during the whole experience. That old familiar sense of
pride I'd felt as a toddler playing T-ball mingled with an
even newer, rewarding feeling of accomplishment. It was in
those moments that I realized how good it could feel to
receive praise and accolades for a job well done. Doing
your best for your own sake is very important, but it's
always nice to receive recognition and feel appreciated.

I was even able to catch fly balls at the home run
tournament; well, let me put it another way, at least I tried to
catch those balls. Although I don't remember actually
catching any (they were coming in fast and furious, and I
was only eight), I had a great time and would always cherish
those memories for years to come.

The media was also very interested in my baseball
career, even as a child. I remember posing for a photo shoot

with my father in our front yard, and being interviewed by a reporter or two. Fun stuff for an eight-year-old; let me tell you.

The Pittsburgh Pirates even invited me and my family to attend some of their home games. We sat in the press box and were treated like royalty. My name appeared on the jumbotron as Jackie Robinson's daughter, Sharon, threw out the first pitch to me. For as much as I can remember, it all seemed like a surreal experience.

When I was about ten years old, my father introduced me to weight training. My mother hated it and was always afraid I would get hurt. She even told me, "It will stunt your growth!" But now, I am six foot eight, and I wonder just how tall I might have gotten! Even though we had a limited amount of equipment, my father made sure we made the most of what we had. He even had other family members lifting weights, and it soon became a competition to see who could be the best. That experience taught me that you don't always have to have the best of everything; you simply have to make the best of what you have.

As I got older, my hitting skills improved in baseball, and I was hitting a lot of home runs, doubles and triples. I continued playing baseball for a few more years, but then switched to only playing football when I started my high school years. I wanted to focus on one sport that I was most passionate about. My father and brother were encouraging me, and working with me to hone my football skills. As a football player, I must confess that even at age three, I got a big kick out of wearing a football helmet and carrying the football around the yard. Little did I realize that I would one day play professional sports.

As I grew older, I started to really appreciate the training that my father had put Devon and myself through. Whether it was running, hitting or catching a ball, I could count on my father to push me "just enough" to make me want to keep moving forward and reach new goals. He believed in me when I thought I could not give any more; he motivated me to keep trying, and to never give up.

I still smile at the thought of those Saturday morning football games when my brother and I were in the Pop Warner league. I truly enjoyed them. My father, because he loved sports so much, was also a coach, and he did some amazing things in his role. He made sure the team had new uniforms, new equipment, and that everyone had a chance to play during a game, even if only briefly. He was a creative coach and developed some of the most strategic plays.

Not to brag too much, but I remember playing on the midget football team, and scoring four touchdowns and making some great plays. On more than one occasion, when our football game was finished, I changed uniforms and played with the next level of teams. It was then and there I realized that people (and by people, I mean my teammates) counted on you to do your very best, every single time you stepped on the field. With that being said, I made sure I gave over one hundred percent, no matter what team I was playing with. That's the beauty of team sports — it feels good to know people are depending on you, but it also requires responsibility. Your teammates are there to encourage you and hold you accountable, and you should always be prepared to do the same for them.

Within a few years, I found myself playing alongside Devon. He was a quarterback, I was a running back/receiver, and my father was a coach. This gave me and my brother ample time to learn the plays and execute them with precision. There were times when Devon and I, when it came to football anyway, even knew what the other was thinking. I worked long and hard to win as many games as possible. I not only prepared during the official practice times, but I also worked at home in the backyard and in the local park as well. Playing between my father and my brother, I quickly became a valuable asset, both on and off the field. In my opinion, that's what makes a player great. Is your work done once you walk off the field? Or are you willing to go the extra mile and do the work others may not want to do? That extra edge is what separates the good from the great. This is what was slowly preparing me for my chance to play football on the professional level.

I remember one time being at our grandmother's house, and I was so excited about an upcoming game on a Saturday morning that I woke up at 4 o'clock in the morning to put on my uniform and my spiked shoes. I was walking around upstairs with my shoes going "clickety clack." I woke my father up, and he reminded me that the game would not start until noon. I tip-toed quietly back into my room, slipped under my bed sheets, and buzzed with silent anticipation for morning to finally come.

In football, I played running back and as a linebacker on the midget team. But because I was such a good player, my father (the coach) would use me wherever there was a need. If the team needed a quarterback or any other position, they knew they could count on me to come through for them.

I was always a good team player, something that I attribute to playing sports with my brother at a young age. As I grew older and started playing sports with other people from all different backgrounds and abilities, I learned the importance of having the right attitude and looking out for my teammates.

As I mentioned, my father had a strong belief in training. If he had his way, my brother and I would have trained all day and all night! While at times it seemed as if we did nothing but training exercises with him, I see now how it has made me a better person…and a better ball player. He would always tell us not to let anyone else "out train you," something that was not likely to happen as long as he was around. Whether it was running early in the morning, or lifting weights all afternoon, my father was dedicated to make sure that we had ample time to be trained. Sometimes we would come home after school at about 3 o'clock, and my father would send us out to run hills. If there was a hill in our neighborhood, we had to run it! It was not unusual to run ten or more hills, take a dinner break, and then go to track practice.

When I was nine I joined the track team to stay in shape and continue training in the football off-season. I surprised everyone, including myself, at just how fast I could run. Running in all of those track meets definitely helped build my skills on the football field as well. Having the opportunity to be on the track team in the summer helped me become a better football player because it improved my speed and running technique. I recall thinking just how great it was to be able to run, sprint and excel at something new. I won awards on the track team as well. When our team competed against other track organizations that had "star runners," it seemed that I was always taking the lead and crossing the finish line before anyone else. I was fortunate that I never sustained any serious injuries, either in track or in football. I give thanks to my coach, Mathis "Boo" Harrison, who really helped me develop in track. Although I will always remember and cherish the experiences of running track, I decided to focus all of my time on football during my high school years.

Looking back, I now realize that my father played a major role in my sports journey. I also appreciate just how important all of those experiences were, and how they laid the framework for my career. Teamwork, honesty, dedication, trust, and loyalty are just a few of the character traits that I attribute to my father and my early years of playing a variety of sports. These lessons did not only serve me in the realm of sports, but they also followed me throughout my personal life as a young boy growing up in Braddock, Pennsylvania.

My Youth Football Program

Sharon Robinson (Jackie Robinson daughter) and I

National Skills Champ 'Way Ahead Of Peers'

DEEPAK KARAMCHETI
Courier Staff Writer

Pittsburgh sports fans have been spoiled by the Pirates expected run for the National League Central division crown, but they "ain't seen nothing yet."

The Bucs, with the lowest payroll in the majors, are not the only success story rising on Pittsburgh's ballparks.

Eight-year-old Wesley Lyons from Elliot, has "brought a house down."

Lyons recently won the national title for the seven- and eight-year-old division of the first Fleer Major League Baseball Diamond Skills, a competition testing the fielding and throwing, running and batting proficiency of more than 383,000 competitors nationwide.

"He's way ahead of his peers," said Lyons' father and coach Wes Lyons Sr. "In a couple more years, he'll be in a league his own."

Lyons, the sole Black winner of the competition, may already be in his own league as his father suggests. In the national finals at baseball's All-Star Game at Jacob's Field in Cleveland, he outscored his closest competitor by 93 points—983 to 890—and would have tied for third in the nine- and 10-year-old division. This past Little League season, Lyons' talents forced him to compete with 10-year-olds rather than kids his own age.

The secret to his age-defying success on the diamond escapes him.

"I don't know," Wes Jr. said softly while watching a videotape of the awards ceremony in Cleveland and twirling a football. "I don't have a secret."

His father replied, "The secret's doing your best even when someone's not looking. Never quit. Never give up."

Like many professional athletes, Lyons took a shine to the media attention he received in Cleveland and later in Pittsburgh when he attended the Pirates July 12 tribute to Jackie Robinson and watched the game from a luxury box at Three Rivers Stadium. He has met such stars as Willie Stargell, Ozzie Smith and Joe Black and his face has appeared in newspapers and on television spots including Fox's "Morning Show."

"It's like he's having his own press conference at eight," said his father.

But unlike many of the high-priced ball players that fill the rosters of today's major leagues, Lyons carries himself with a quiet charm, answering questions in a "yes sir/no sir" fashion, letting others do the bragging.

"To make it to the team championship and to make it to the national championship means you're the best," said Eric Curry, project manager with Universal Marketing Association in Atlanta who promoted the event.

The Diamond Skills Challenge took place in four stages—local, sectional, regional and national—all of which Lyons won. Curry noted that Lyons scored the lowest of the four competitors who qualified for the national finals.

"He picked the right day to have a day," Curry said.

Lyons, who formerly attended Shaffer Elementary and will attend Rankin Intermediate next year, has not only seen success on the diamond, but has other athletic skills as well. An orange belt in karate, Lyons won the East Coast Regionals for the seven and under division. In track, he is a standout in the 100-, 200-, 400- and 800-meter races.

"I think he's a better football player," Wes Sr. said of his halfback and middle linebacker son.

After winning the Diamond Skills Challenge and continuing a regimen of practice and weightlifting, Wes Jr. hopes to one day play in the majors for the Seattle Mariners with his favorite player Ken Griffey Jr. But maybe with a little bit of coaxing we will one day see him striding to the plate in Pirate black and gold.

THE CHAMP—Wes Lyons Jr. poses with his father and coach, Wes at their Elliot home. Wes Jr. won the national title of the Fleer/Major League Baseball Diamond Skills competition for seven- and eight-year-olds.

PHOTO BY TRACI WATT

SLUGGER—Eight-year-old Wes Lyons Jr. of Elliot exhibited his abilities by winning the national Fleer/Major League Baseball Diamond Skills competition held at the All-Star Game in Cleveland.

PHOTO BY TRACI WATT

Growing up in Pittsburgh

CHAPTER TWO

"For God has not given us a spirit of timidity, but of power
and love and discipline"
-2 Timothy 1:7

As I look back on my childhood years growing up in

Pittsburgh, it was only fitting that I had an opportunity to

play for the Pittsburgh Steelers. What better sense of pride

than to suit-up in the black and gold that you and your entire

hometown cheered for on game days? Each day I thank the

good Lord for all of the blessings, challenges and

opportunities that I experienced growing up. Every situation

that came my way was preparing me to become the young

man I am now.

To most people, when you say the word

"Pittsburgh," they think of a city containing nothing, but

steel mills and blue collar workers. But to me, Pittsburgh

was always just my home. My world revolved around my family, my friends, athletics and most importantly school.

My brother, Devon, and I were raised in a split home, and divided the time we spent with our mother and father. Every Tuesday and Thursday we went over to my father's house, along with every other weekend, and I have great memories from both homes. Most people do not realize how difficult it can be at times for children who grow up in this type of situation. Kids who have been through it understand that it can be a challenge, emotionally and logistically, to go back and forth. But we made the best out of everything, no matter where we were.

The two houses were on the opposite sides of town, and about a thirty minute drive from each other. One benefit of essentially living in "two places" was having so many friends. We had our friends in our mother's part of town, and a different set of friends in the neighborhood where our father lived.

Looking back, I now realize that being so busy in two neighborhoods actually kept me out of trouble. It seemed like there was always something going on. Whether it was homework around the kitchen table, or playing baseball or football with my friends; there was never a dull moment! I wonder if my brother and I would have followed down a different path: hanging out on the street corner and eventually dealing drugs (like some people we knew) if we had not been so busy and involved in our communities. To this day, that is why I encourage youth to discover their passion and pursue it whole-heartedly. Not only is it a positive way to stay out of trouble, but just imagine the places it can take you, whether it be on the turf as you make your first play in a Sunday Night Football game or in the corner office of a corporate Hi-Rise as you preside over a Fortune 500 company. A little self-discipline and healthy dose of passion can go a long way.

My mother's house was not located in the best of neighborhoods, but she made sure that my brother and I did not hang out with the "wrong crowd." It was not unusual to see drug dealers on the street corners all hours of the day and night, along with crack heads and junkies roaming the streets at will. Both of my parents made sure that Devon and I led a positive and productive path so we were not distracted by the negative influences of this neighborhood. My father would call and remind us about practicing when we were at our mother's house. He was on a mission to keep us busy and active; that's for sure!

The contrast between growing up at my mother's house compared to my father's house was almost as different as night and day. I attended the school district where my mother's house was located. Her main focus, while I was growing up, was for me to excel in school and have a relationship with God. My mother, Marva Lamar, is the one who introduced me to my Lord and savior, Jesus Christ, at a really young age. Faith is the reason why I have been able to stay motivated. It has truly helped me get through some of the toughest times in my life. I've found that faith can really help serve as a spiritual compass, for painful times when you can't seem to find help or hope elsewhere, and I believe my faith has also been the reason for so many blessings in my life.

My father's house seemed to be more structured around sports and physical fitness, which definitely laid the foundation for who I am today as an athlete. Although juggling two homes is challenging for most people, I must admit that I enjoyed the differences in the schedules: at my mother's house, she was more lenient and allowed me to go outside and play after school (and I recall a few times trying not to be around in case my father were to call and give me my "marching orders"). Don't get me wrong, my mother would lay down the law if she had to; especially if I tried to go outside before finishing my homework.

For the most part, Devon helped to keep me out of trouble. While we would occasionally see one of our friends steal candy from a store, or pick up a bike they saw on the street, I always knew the difference between right and wrong. I never even thought about crossing the line and joining them.

In school, math was my favorite subject. I had a teacher named Mr. Leith who went above and beyond the call of duty to not only make sure that math was interesting to learn, but also that all of his students understood the lessons. I enjoyed the subject so much that I even went to his class before school started to earn extra credit for doing some additional math problems. I was always a curious student in school; if I did not understand something, I made sure that there was someone to help me along the way. There's nothing wrong with asking questions —the best way to learn and grow is to find out the answers to things you don't know. That applies on and off the field.

My brother and I were, and still are, very close. He was a role model to me growing up and he always tried his best to look after me. I recall one time playing "follow the leader," I followed him through an opening in the steps…and my head got stuck! He had to get our mother to come to the rescue; it was kind of embarrassing at the time, but at least he did not abandon me when it happened. That is just one of the many memories that we have together, which shows how Devon has helped to keep me out of harm's way (or tried, anyway!).

Another great memory I have with my brother is building "couch forts" in our mother's basement. The basement seemed ideal for two active boys who were not afraid to flip over a couch or chair and make their own little forts. We had some great times playing in the basement; some might even call it our own "fortress of solitude." When we weren't building our couch forts, we were off wrestling with one another. We have always had a lot in common, and I guess that is why we've been able to get along so well.

Once in a blue moon I might have gotten mad about something, and I know I was tempted to reach out and hit him…but I don't recall any times that we actually fought. Of course, we are brothers, and at times we would have a verbal disagreement over something silly, like what television show we were going to watch, etc., but that was the simple extent of our bickering.

At an early age, I received a lot of support from my grandparents when I was playing sports. My father's parents, Mary and Howard, whom Devon and I fondly referred to as Nana and Pap Pap — seemed to be my own personal cheerleading squad. I could always count on them to attend every sporting event that I played in. Whether it was football, baseball, a track meet or anything else, I could always count on them being there. It did not matter if it was raining or cold; they were there to support me. I admit that it also helped to instill confidence and self-esteem in me over the years, and for their support, I am forever grateful to them.

When I was about ten years old, my Pap Pap passed away. He used to always call me "Speedy" when I was little, and I can still hear his voice yelling "Go Speedy!" Even though my grandfather had passed, it never stopped my Nana from continuing to show up at my games to support and encourage me. Just thinking about them can always put a smile on my face.

Other family members also supported me as I was growing up, especially when it came to sporting events. My

stepmother was always there to cheer me on, as well as a
few of my uncles, who still call me "Speedy" to this day.
My mother and her mother, Robbie, tried to attend my
games as often as they could, and I could always count on
them for a smile and a hug. My cousins, brother, step sister,
and even some of my friends (from both neighborhoods)
came to my games and were also part of my support system.
At that time, and as a child, I didn't really give any of this a
second thought. After all, when you are that young, you just
expect family and friends to come to your games. But
looking back, I realize how all of those people in my life
were giving up their time and making a big effort to support
me. Every now and then, I really do miss those times. It
was a great blessing for me to have the support of my family
and friends.

Splitting our lives between two homes was not too
bad for my brother and me for the most part. Sometimes the
weeks would seem to fly by, and at other times, they
dragged on. We had a group of friends from each
neighborhood, and we enjoyed spending time and playing
sports with them. Of course, this was when my father was
not keeping me too busy with training, grass cutting and
running hills. Still, those exciting childhood years in

Pittsburgh prepared me for the next big chapter of my life —
high school!

Grandparents and I

High School Years

"When you can do the common things of life in an uncommon way, you will command the attention of the world."

- George Washington Carver

Throughout my entire life, my father has always been my football coach. He started training me when I first started to walk, and he has seen me through both the hard and the best times. No one knew me better than he did. If it were not for his dedication, discipline, hard work and a "never give up" mentality, I really don't think that I would have made it thus far in sports. Despite his ways of instilling fear into my brother and me (as a way of motivating us), I knew he loved us and just wanted us to achieve something bigger and better in life. I will always owe my father gratitude and thanks for all of these reasons and more.

Having someone else coach me when I started playing high school football felt odd at first, but it gave me more freedom, which helped me to quickly adjust. It also allowed me to develop and grow into my own personality. I became more outgoing and I developed my own style of play.

As you can imagine, having your father as your football coach can be both a blessing and a curse at times. It was difficult to separate the "parent" from the "coach," which made me uptight from time to time. My father had a hard time letting go, and he even showed up at many of my football practice sessions in high school. So, while I was somewhat relaxed, I still had to be on my toes (and on my best behavior) because I knew he was watching my every move.

My faith has also helped guide me through my career, especially while in school. Peer pressure from all sides can sometimes steer a teenager down the wrong path, but my faith in the Lord kept me on the straight and narrow. My faith, and my parents, helped me stay focused, no matter what I was trying to accomplish.

Similarly, I have always believed in having a positive attitude. There is a saying that goes "your attitude

is your most prized possession," and I believe this to be true.
Having the right attitude can make all of the difference in
the world between success and failure, especially when
things are looking bleak.

As I mentioned before, I attended the school district
in my mother's neighborhood of Woodland Hills.
Woodland Hills School District created a lot of fond
memories for me. There are 12 different neighborhoods that
make up the Woodland Hills area, and this allowed us to
have one big and very bad (in a good way) football team. It
was, and still is, a football powerhouse.

Our football team played at a stadium called "The
Wolvarena." In 2001, *USA Today* voted "The Wolvarena"
as one of the top 10 best places to watch a high school
football game in the country, and the stadium was also once
voted as the "most intimidating stadium" in Pennsylvania.
With a reputation like this, it is no surprise that Woodland
Hills produced phenomenal athletes. All of the players
worked well together: we trained hard, and we played hard.
We had the attitude of winners, and it showed on the playing
field. Woodland Hills has been supplying the NFL teams
with numerous players over the years. *USA Football*
announced that Woodland Hills High School had the most

NFL players in 2010, and as of this writing, I believe a large number of former Woodland Hills players are still on the rosters of NFL teams today.

There were always large crowds of supporters at our sporting events in Woodland Hills, and that gives you a good feeling when you are playing on the team. On the other hand, it also gives you a little pressure to do your best (which, in retrospect, is probably a good thing)...because you don't want to disappoint your fans and supporters who follow your every move on a regular basis.

Football is a team sport, and everyone on the team, no matter how often they get to play in the actual games, is just as important as the next guy. There were always a great bunch of teammates who had my back throughout my time playing football for Woodland Hills. There were no "big egos" on the team. Instead, we were a group of football players who knew we were on a mission: to play our very best and win! And win we did.

In the 2006 season, another player named Darrin Walls and I were the star players for Woodland Hills. We won awards and were highly recruited, which helped keep Woodland Hills in the spotlight. It seemed as if we were always being profiled or interviewed by the local media outlets. It's not unusual to hear about star athletes who think that their talent will get them into college rather than working hard both on and off the field. However, between my faith, my teammates, my brother and all the guidance from my parents, I was able to handle it very well.

I will never forget my senior year when the Woodland Hills football team was ranked number one by a certain newspaper, but Gateway (our biggest rival in 2005) was ranked number one by a different newspaper. Talk about having to live up to high expectations! A week prior to when we would face each other, Darrin and I were able to actually see Gateway's football team in action against a school from Ohio. We had our Woodland Hills jerseys on, and some of the Gateway spectators started yelling stuff like, "we'll beat you next week!"

We did not let that bother us; we were only there to see a rival football team in action. A week later when our team and Gateway met, it was a blow out. Darrin and I both scored two touchdowns, and celebrated as we showed everyone in western Pennsylvania who the number one team truly was. In high-pressure situations like that one, it's important to stay focused and practice mind control. We could have easily let the jeers from the opposing team's fans or the critiques of local media trick us into doubting our abilities. But it is in those moments that it helps to remember all of your prior successes, the hard work and preparation you've done, and the family and fans that are on your side regardless of the outcome.

During my high school years, my fan base was made up of family, friends, neighbors, alumni and other folks from the general area who loved to support local teams. Between the pep rallies, bonfires, and the actual games, it was easy to fall into the "look at me, I'm the best player on the team" syndrome, which is a very dangerous way for a teenager to think. I recall a time when I received a drawing in high school from an elementary kid who looked up to me as a football player. This was just the beginning of me becoming a role model for other people. It helped inspire me to continue to excel and do my very best, both in school and on the field.

The competition between my brother and I became pretty intense with all of this high school fame. Of course, we were both pretty talented, so getting scholarships was not really a challenge. At one point, I thought I would earn more scholarship offers than my brother, who earned over sixty, but that never really happened. When my brother ended up selecting Ohio State, some of the recruiters thought that I would automatically pick that college as well, and they didn't bother to try and entice me to their school.

Breaking records is something that both my brother and I were able to accomplish. I currently hold the record for the most receiving yards and receptions in Woodland Hills history. I was able to accomplish this and many other goals because of all the training that I received from my father. The determination that he infused in my brother and me allowed us to go the extra distance and be better than most players in high school.

To this day, I still keep in touch with some of the teachers and coaches at Woodland Hills. I have even had speaking engagements at the schools to help encourage and motivate the students on many occasions. I graduated from high school in 2006, and I was able to close the door on this chapter in my life with a sense of accomplishment and pride. I had a pretty good idea of what would lie ahead for me in college, thanks to my older brother (who never seemed to mind blazing a trail for me to follow). I knew I had plenty of opportunities moving forward, and I wanted to take full advantage of every experience that came with the life of a college football player.

Family

Kid Drawing

Central Catholic focus keying on Wolverines

GAME, FROM PAGE EZ-11

114-16.

"It is Central-Woodland Hills," first-year Central Catholic coach Terry Totten said. "I don't think all that much more needs to be said."

True.

This is "the game" on the high school slate in this, a week busting at the seems with quality matchups around the region.

And the Central Catholic defense knows it will have to deal with a couple of the WPIAL's most explosive components when the Wolverines step up to the football in their signature "Michigan" helmets.

These Wolverines feature 6-foot-5, 205-pound receiver Wes Lyons, who has shown that he can go vertical on a defense as well as use his skill to sit down in the middle, just behind the linebackers. Woodland Hills coach George Novak also has Darrin Walls. Cornerback Walls, who recently announced he'll attend Notre Dame, has also shined for the Woodland Hills offense and at 6 feet 1, 175 pounds, can play both receiver and running back.

"I've noticed those kids at combine camps and just from hearing about them and playing against them in the past," said Nate Williams, a Central Catholic senior linebacker who is garnering interest from Big Ten schools.

"I know how athletic those guys are and what they can do. We have to limit them and I think everyone knows that."

Much like any successful defense, everything must start up front for Central Catholic if the Vikings are going to contain the powder keg Woodland Hills offense. Central Catholic brutes Pat Illig, Stefan Wisniewski and Quentin Williams are guys that Totten is counting on to get that surge into the Wolverines backfield.

"Our pass rush is always a big part of the defense," Illig said. "That's something that is going to be really big in this game. We have to get their quarterback frazzled in the pocket if we can."

So there it is, the goal clearly defined, the Central Catholic defense the unit in the WPIAL most likely under a microscope this week.

"We know they are going to be ready, they are a top-notch football team," Totten said of Woodland Hills.

"It is a matter of us getting ourselves to that same level. If you let down a second, they have the ability to take it to the house on any play."

Matt Freed/Post-Gazette

Woodland Hills' Wes Lyons pulls down a touchdown between Gateway's Brandon Livsey, left, and Aaron Smith Sept. 2.

HIGH SCHOOL FOOTBALL
ScoutingReport

PLAYER TO WATCH

Wes Lyons

Woodland Hills' super-sized receiver a threat.

GAME	DAY	TIME	WHAT YOU SHOULD KNOW
WPIAL CLASS AAAA			
Norwin (1-5, 1-3) at Penn Hills (5-1, 3-1)	Tomorrow	7:30 p.m.	Penn Hills quarterback Chad Parker has completed 42 of 80 passes for 762 yards, 7 TDs.
Penn-Trafford (1-5, 0-4) at Hempfield (1-5, 0-4)	Tomorrow	7:30 p.m.	The winner will move out of the Quad East Conference cellar.
Woodland Hills (6-0, 4-0) at Central Catholic (5-1, 4-0)	Tomorrow	7:30 p.m.	The winner takes over sole possession of first place in the Quad East Conference.
Kiski Area (2-4, 2-2) at Plum (1-5, 0-3)	Tomorrow	7:30 p.m.	Plum QB Gino Ron elfo has completed 70 of 151 passes for 872 yards and 7 TDs.
Latrobe (0-3, 3-3) at McKeesport (4-1, 3-0)	Tomorrow	7:30 p.m.	Latrobe has been outscored 104-21 in three Quad Southwest Conference games.
Thomas Jefferson (6-0) at Gateway (5-1)	Tomorrow	7:30 p.m.	Thomas Jefferson, No. 1 in Class AAA, is averaging 48.5 points per game.
WPIAL CLASS AAA			
Franklin Regional (5-1, 3-1) at Knoch (2-4, 1-2)	Tomorrow	7:30 p.m.	Franklin Regional RB Ronny Armstrong has gained 812 yards with 12 TDs on 84 carries.
Albert Gallatin (3-3, 3-1) at Yough (5-1, 4-0)	Tomorrow	7:30 p.m.	Yough leads the Keystone Conference. Albert Gallatin is tied with Laurel Highlands for second.
Derry Area (1-5, 1-3) at Uniontown (3-3, 2-2)	Tomorrow	7:30 p.m.	Uniontown QB Steve Kuzmansky completed 53 of 126 passes for 746 yards and 6 TDs.
Greensburg Salem (3-5, 1-3) at Laurel Highlands (3-3, 3-1)	Tomorrow	7:30 p.m.	Greensburg Salem QB Josh Williams has completed 40 of 99 passes for 827 yards, 4 TDs.
WPIAL CLASS AA			
Deer Lakes (2-4, 1-3) at Burrell (5-1, 3-1)	Tomorrow	7:30 p.m.	Burrell RB Tyler Henderson has rushed for 877 yards and 13 TDs on 94 carries.
Ford City (5-1, 4-0) at Valley (4-2, 4-0)	Tomorrow	7:30 p.m.	The winner takes over sole possession of first place in the Allegheny Conference.
Greensburg C.C. (5-0, 4-0) at Waynesburg (2-4, 1-3)	Tomorrow	7:30 p.m.	Greensburg C.C. is averaging 50.2 points per game and allowing only 4.4 per game.
McGuffey (4-2, 4-0) at Jeannette (6-0, 4-0)	Tomorrow	7:30 p.m.	McGuffey and Jeannette are tied with Greensburg C.E. for the Interstate Conference lead.
Washington (4-2, 2-2) at East Allegheny (1-5, 0-4)	Tomorrow	7:30 p.m.	Washington could be without coach Bill Britton for a second week, due to teachers strike.
WPIAL CLASS A			
Wilkinsburg (0-6, 0-4) at Clairton (2-4, 2-2)	Tomorrow	7:30 p.m.	Wilkinsburg has lost 11 of its last 12 games dating back to last season.
Apollo-Ridge (2-4, 2-2) at Riverview (3-3, 2-2)	Saturday	2 p.m.	Apollo-Ridge and Riverview are in a four-way tie with Serra and Clairton for the lead in Eastern Conference.
Leechburg (0-6, 0-4) at Serra Catholic (4-2, 2-2)	Saturday	7:30 p.m.	Serra RB Isiah Jackson has rushed for 812 yards and 6 TDs on 110 carries.
CITY LEAGUE			
Langley (3-2, 3-2) at Schenley (3-3, 2-2)	Tonight	7 p.m.	Schenley returns to City League play after last week's 35-14 nonconference loss to Seton-LaSalle.
Brashear (3-2, 3-2) at Westinghouse (0-4, 0-4)	Saturday	Noon	Westinghouse has lost nine consecutive City League games dating back to last season.
Allderdice (2-3, 2-2) at Peabody (2-3, 2-3)	Saturday	3:30 p.m.	Peabody's Ryan Bailey threw for 264 yards and ran for a TD in last week's 44-6 loss to Brashear.

PITTSBURGH TRIBUNE-REVIEW HIGH SCHOOLS · BOXING MONDA'

HIGH SCHOOLS

Lyons grows into starring role

The 6-foot-6 receiver hopes to escape his brother's shadow and set Woodland Hills receiving records.

BY KEVIN GORMAN
TRIBUNE-REVIEW

The pass, as Woodland Hills coach George Novak remembers it, sailed 12 feet high and into the end zone.

Wes Lyons reached above the crossbar of the goal post and snatched it with one hand before landing.

"Jaws dropped at West Virginia University's passing camp," especially the one attached to the face of Mountaineers coach Rich Rodriguez, standing nearby.

"That," Novak said, "was unbelievable."

With that catch, the 6-foot-6, 205-pound Lyons officially stepped out of his brother's shadow and solidified his own reputation as a high-major college prospect. No longer was he living on the borrowed reputation of Devon Lyons, an Ohio State sophomore.

"Coach Rodriguez was right there at that goal post," Lyons said. "It was right in front of him and the other coaches. They already knew I had potential, but that shocked him."

Wes Lyons broke Ryan Mundy's school record for receptions for a junior with 33 for 563 yards and six touchdowns, but many in football circles were shocked to hear that he had received scholarship offers from national powers Miami and Oklahoma.

Novak credits Lyons' bottomless potential — he doesn't turn 17 until September and is just starting to fill out his frame — and work ethic for the increased interest.

Lyons follows an intense workout regimen, which includes jumping onto 36-inch plyometric boxes while wearing two, 10-pound weighted vests to improve his leg strength and explosiveness.

"He's had a phenomenal offseason," Novak said. "He's done a great job lifting and worked real hard on his running. He has outstanding hand-eye coordination. And he's just

He's just a pony."

Still, Wes Lyons can't escape comparisons to Devon (6-4, 215), who was shorter, thicker and faster, capable of running reverses and returning punts. Wes is long, lean and a big threat on deep routes and corner fades.

"They're different personalities," Novak said of the Lyons brothers. "Wes has very deceptive speed. He's smooth, and

CHRISTOPHER HORNER/TRIBUNE-REVIEW

Woodland Hills receiver Wes Lyons catches a pass last week at the Wolverines' training camp near Ligonier.

Getting ready

This is the eighth in a series of player profiles that the Pittsburgh Tribune-Review will be running leading up to the start of the football season.

One, as Lyons proved at West Virginia, who is capable of going up to great heights to

Wes Lyons

School: Woodland Hills
Height, weight: 6-foot-6, 205 pounds
Class: Senior
Position: Receiver
Notable: Lyons has nearly two dozen scholarship offers and counts Miami, Ohio State, Oklahoma and

Recruiting Process

CHAPTER FOUR

"Be strong and courageous. Do not fear or be in dread of
them, for it is the LORD your God who goes with you. He
will not leave you or forsake you."
- Deuteronomy 31:6

Now looking back, one of the best times in my life was

transitioning from a high school to a college athlete. This

process started when I was a sophomore in high school. As

a sophomore, I knew what was expected by my parents in

school and on the football field. I held over a 3.0 grade

point average and started some football games as a

sophomore. Mid-way through my sophomore season, I

began to receive letters from top college programs. The

arrival of the letters marked the beginning of the recruitment

process, which was not an unfamiliar path for me, since my

brother and cousin, Ryan Mundy, went through the same

process a couple years before me. As I finished the season of my sophomore year, my brother, Devon, was one of the top recruits as a senior, earning over 60 Division I college offers and later signing to The Ohio State University. Just like in our early days of playing outside together or building couch forts in the house, my friendly competitiveness with my brother kicked in. I wanted to earn more than he ever did, but I clearly had my work cut out of me.

For many, the recruitment process is a mysterious one, young athletes often wonder how it works or ask me what they can expect. Well, leading up to my junior year in high school, I began to get heavily recruited. Calls were coming in every night. Whether it was news reporters or college coaches, they were calling nonstop. This all made me feel important. However, it was annoying at times since I would receive up to ten calls a night in many cases. My schedule had to be balanced because I had to manage going to school, then going to practice, followed by getting homework completed, and ending with calls from recruiters at night. There was very little time for play, but that was a sacrifice that I was willing to make to be successful.

Not too long after my junior season, scholarships started coming in on a weekly basis. On the same day, I received my first scholarships from West Virginia University (WVU) and Boston College. This was a great feeling! I knew that I was going to college for free and a huge weight was lifted off of my shoulders — even better, it made me happy to know that my parents would not have to worry about struggling to pay for either one of their sons' education. Many more scholarships were to follow. As the rest of the school year went on, I knew it was time to take the SAT exam. Once I passed this test, I was assured that I was going to college. This was one of the final hurdles that I needed to overcome to get me to the next level.

I would have to say that the college visits were my favorite part throughout this recruiting process. I visited colleges all over the country. The recruitment period was a wonderful time to travel and really enjoy the schools I was visiting. With West Virginia University being only an hour away, I had attended games since I was a freshman in high school. Leading into my senior year, I was very interested in The University of Miami, where my good friend, Darrin, my father and I traveled on an unofficial visit. I was very tempted to commit to that college, but it was too early since I had over a half a year before signing day. I was also very interested in The Ohio State University (OSU) because it was a place that I visited almost every week since Devon went to college there: I even stayed there for a couple of weeks in the summer to spend time with him. Deciding where I was going to spend the next four years was a big decision that needed to be made and, at that time, I had seen all of the colleges; I was almost ready to make a choice.

Visiting colleges was not the only thing that I was impressed by during this process; I was also impressed by the many coaches that came to visit. As a senior, I was rated as one of the top athletes in Pennsylvania. Coaches would come to my games, school, and even homes too. A couple of times a week, I would be called into the office during the school day to meet with college coaches from universities such as USC, LSU, WVU and OSU etc. Similarly, I would have coaches visiting my home throughout the week as well. Those exciting times felt reminiscent of those early moments as a child playing baseball, when I'd first felt the thrill of recognition for my hard work. I recall the entire West Virginia University offensive coaching staff coming to visit, including the head coach. This made WVU stick out in the recruiting process, plus they were very friendly and showed me how bad they wanted me by coming to visit every week. One of the coolest things that stuck out about the WVU coaches was that they would play video games with me, and we bonded on so many levels. College would be my first time stepping away from my parent's protection and safety net. I wanted a place where I would feel welcome, understood, and at home.

These meetings were not only about fun and games, but they were also about business. We discussed where I would fit in on the team, and how I would contribute as a freshman, which was very important to me. They told me things like, "I would start immediately, they would be there for me if I needed anything throughout my four years," and they expressed how they would change their offense and throw over fifty times a game (as a wide receiver that sounded great) if I were to choose to attend WVU. Although at the time I did not realize it, these were just words being spoken to get me to commit.

The Ohio State University was my favorite school ever since my brother was being recruited. Coach Tressell was doing great things with the Ohio State program and he showed interest in me, while he was trying to convince my brother to commit. My brother and I were very close, and when he decided to attend OSU, it made the college even more favorable for me to want to commit there. I thought of all the benefits of me going there:

- I would have my brother around
- It would be easy on my parents
- And it felt as if I knew everyone since I spent so much time there

With the time running out and my decision making time getting closer, the schools started to make their final stance. Ohio State and West Virginia were my top choices. My mother left this decision completely up to me. It didn't matter where I went to college, she was just happy because my education would be free. My father was very helpful in the decision process. He was a great negotiator and made a deal with WVU. The agreement was that my step sister would also have a full scholarship to attend WVU with me if I were to commit to them. This was a great opportunity for her to earn a great education, without getting into debt as well.

With all of the scholarship offers on the table, I came together with my parents and made the best decision. I had a press conference where top athletes, media, friends and family all attended. We had dinner and made this press conference into an event. Leading up to the press conference, I heard about bets being made on where I would attend college, as if this were a Vegas prize fight. The buzz was building in our community and I couldn't wait to reveal my big decision at the press conference. As I announced that I would attend college at West Virginia University, I had a big airbrushed shirt with a WV logo on it hidden away. As the cheers began, I pulled that shirt out and wore it with pride the rest of the day.

This was the most important decision I would ever make in my life and I chose WVU for so many reasons. Ohio State has a great program, but it was time for me to step out of my brother's shadow and explore the country roads of West Virginia. I was so excited to begin a journey at WVU. I loved that it was close to my home so my family could travel to see me play every week without a problem. I knew that the coaches and players would treat me like family and welcome me to the team. I was eager to play as a true freshman, which a lot of football players didn't have the opportunity to do. I could not wait to come through the tunnel at Milan Puskar Stadium on Saturdays and feel the momentum from the music playing and fans cheering us on. I was blessed to officially be a Mountaineer.

The day I signed to WVU

Recruiting visit to the University of Miami

Wesley Lyons - Pittsburgh
9 videos available »

COLLEGE CHOICES

School	Interest	Offer	Visit	Recruited by
West Virginia	COMMITTED (01/26/2006)	✓	09/30/2005	Tony Gibson
Boston Coll.	None	✓	10/07/2005	Jim Bridge
Louisville	None	✓	None	
Miami (FL)	None	✓	None	
Ohio St.	None	✓	10/14/2005	Joe Daniels

Adapting to College

CHAPTER FIVE

"For I know the plans I have for you," says the Lord.
"They are plans for good and not for disaster, to give you a
future and a hope."
- Jeremiah 29:11

One week after I graduated high school, I reported to

campus at West Virginia University (WVU). After getting a

physical, I started the summer workout with the rest of the

team. I was one of the three freshmen who had reported for

summer training early. My new teammates and coaches

seemed to be interested in me since I was the biggest wide

receiver on the team — I stood at 6'6" and weighed nearly

220 pounds. I was only 17 at the time and most players

were in their 20s. I will never forget my first workout as a

Mountaineer. I was thrown into the fire with the veteran

players.

Mike was our strength coach and he was the toughest guy I had ever met. Mike reminded me of a world champion UFC fighter. The first time I entered the facility where we trained, my heart was beating fast and I had butterflies. We started off by lifting weights, which was normal to me since my best friend, Kirk, and I lifted weights with my father daily prior to my arrival to WVU. Next, we began to do agility drills (box jumps, jump rope, etc.) between our weight lifting sets. After about two hours of this, I was really fatigued and couldn't wait to lie down. Every muscle in my body hurt, but the workout wasn't over. We still had to run.

Running has never been a huge challenge for me since I was a track runner. However, the Mountaineer way of running is much more than "just running!" We had to run until our legs felt as if they were going to fall off. We ran sprints that were timed and if we missed our set time, we had to make up each sprint that we missed. If we bent over to touch our knees, we had to do an extra sprint. At times, there was no set number of sprints we had to run, we just ran until Mike was satisfied. The trainers took me out one sprint as I began to lag behind since this was my first workout. Unfortunately, veteran players could not sit out and were forced to keep going. These intense workouts often pushed many players to the point of exhaustion — they could not go on and fell out. Not only is the workout strenuous, but it was also really hot outside. As some of the players fell out, Mike would curse at them, make them get up, and tell them to keep running. This workout regimen sometimes led to players quitting the team. Finally, Mike stopped us because he saw that barely anyone was making the times. I still wonder if Mike's goal was to kill us or make us stronger. I assume it is the latter because I lived to tell the story.

After all of the running on my first day of practice, players still had to make up every sprint that they missed. This made the team very hostile and irritable. As we were making up sprints, it began to rain. All I remember hearing was Selvish Capers and Berry Wright, the biggest two players on the team, yelling at one another. Next thing you know, a fight broke out! I had never witnessed anything like this from teammates before and I removed myself from the situation, while other players such as Pat White and Steve Slaton tried to stop these big, athletic, 300-pound men. Eventually Mike ran in and put one of the guys in a hold so he couldn't move and the players grabbed the other guy. This was an interesting start to my college experience. As I returned home, I asked myself, "What did I get myself into?" Fortunately for me, the workouts began to get easier, as I adapted to the work load.

As the blazing summer days dwindled away, we began to see our coaches more often as they returned from vacation. In one of the first meetings for freshmen only, I remember the coaches saying that all of the recruiting stuff they told us was lies. They felt it was okay to tell us that, since our parents were then out of the picture. I felt somewhat deceived, but I had planned on working hard to earn everything that was promised. The coaches made it seem as if we belonged to them, and as a freshman, I felt as if I did. That was one meeting that I would never forget.

Freshmen have the hardest schedule to follow. We take the most classes compared to the other players. The strategy behind this is for freshman to remain eligible to participate in athletics even if we perform poorly in one or two classes. The transition from high school to college can often be a huge adjustment for any student, so the coaches tried their best to provide a cushion for freshman in case there were any issues with our classes. Our daily schedule included the following agenda:

- Class from 8am until 2pm, with a lunch break
- Football meetings from 2:30pm until 4pm
- Football practice 4:30pm until 6:30pm
- Dinner at 7pm
- Study hall from 7pm until 9pm

This schedule didn't leave much time for goofing off, which made me grow up and get my first taste of an adult life. Everything that I did was going to be my decision; whether I wanted to stay up late, party on a school night, go to class or even go to practice. Even though I was free to make the wrong decision, there would be consequences if I were to miss any of the items on the above schedule.

Out of all the requirements, missing class had the biggest repercussion. There were people (spies) whose job was to check each football player's classes daily. These people would sit in your class and report to your coach if you came or not, if you were late, or if you left early. For every class we missed, we would get tortured by pushing 45 pound plates, and do buddy carries (carrying someone on your back) up and down the field after practice. Fortunately for myself, I was disciplined and wanted to make a good impression on the coaches so I never missed any classes.

Self-discipline is important for any young adult, whether or not you are a student athlete. Although it can be tempting to take the easy way out, it is important to remember your long-term goals and how your short-term decisions may influence your ability to reach them. If I had gotten on my coaches bad side or flunked out of school, where would I be today? Certainly not where I was aiming to be.

Making good impressions was easy for me since I was raised to be well mannered, but I felt it was something I had to do way too often. I had three wide receiver coaching changes in my four years at WVU. This is hard for any player, especially when you connect with the coach who recruited you. Butch Jones was my first coach, and he was part of the reason that I chose to attend West Virginia. He was offered a head coach job that he couldn't pass up after my freshman year. I wasn't mad about it at the time, but it was definitely hard to see him go after I built such a strong relationship with him. He was someone who I expected to be there for me throughout my four years of college. I was disappointed, but this was the first time that I realized the business of football. As a high school student athlete, you never expect or consider the possibility that the coaches who recruited you will leave, but once you are placed in this position, you learn to adjust and move forward.

I decided to focus on the positive aspects of transitioning from a high school to college athlete. There was a huge difference between traveling on a school bus to high school games and how the team traveled in college. We stayed in a hotel together whether the game was at home or away. This structure allowed our team to be close and create a brotherly bond. The team flew as a unit on private planes to our away games. Seniors had it the best because they flew in the first class seating. I was usually seated next to one of the big linemen in the exit row to allow for extra leg room. As we landed at a private airport, there would be four buses waiting for us, along with police escorts to guide us to our luxury hotel where we would stay. The way the police escorts drove alongside our buses so we could get to our destination in a timely fashion made me feel like I was traveling with the president.

When we arrived at the hotel, we would have a couple of hours free, then a voluntary Fellowship of Christian Athletes (FCA) meeting, followed by dinner. We all did different activities during our free time at the hotel. We would cut each other's hair, watch movies, nap, wrestle, and even play tricks on each other. After dinner, we had meetings, some more free time, and then another meeting to watch a highlight tape of our previous game. Each player's goal was to make great plays to end up on the highlight tape because these highlight tapes got everyone excited and ready to play. I loved the camaraderie and excitement that we had before every game.

The best trips we took were when we traveled to our bowl games. We stayed at beautiful five star resorts. We did the same things we would do for a regular game, but it was for an extended period of time. We received great gifts just for going to the game — things like TVs, watches, gift cards and other electronics. The times we won, we received a bowl ring, which I would cherish forever.

Like any transition, adapting to college had its good and bad moments. However, the good times definitely outweighed the bad. I was able to triumph through the workouts, class schedules, coaching changes and every other challenge that came in my direction that year, as well as enjoy the luxuries of being a freshman football player at WVU. Everything that I went through was a learning experience that helped me become a stronger person.

Life as a Mountaineer

CHAPTER SIX

But Jesus looked at them and said, "With man this is impossible, but with God all things are possible."
- Matthew 19:26

Some of the best moments of my life occurred when I attended West Virginia University (WVU). For me, it was not just a college where I once played football, it was a second home where I developed into the man that I am today. From leisurely outdoor strolls in between classes to the contagious energy of campus on game days, there are a lot of memories I cherish. It is a place that had irreplaceable fans, tremendous team support, and remarkable academics. These were the reasons that I decided to join WVU compared to many other universities that offered scholarships to me.

When I went to my first WVU game while I was a
freshman in high school, I instantly knew that I could see
myself playing football there. Fans mean the world to
football players and I was fortunate enough to attend WVU,
where there were the best fans in all of the college sports.
The Mountaineer football team belonged to more than just
the university. It was a statewide camaraderie between the
university and the residents of West Virginia. WVU always
had a reputation for having loyal fans that support all of
their sports and activities. It didn't matter whether they
lived over four or five hours away, these fans would travel
to watch WVU football games each week to show their
support. Additionally, it was not unusual to see fans
camping out the night before, just so they could purchase
tickets and grab a great spot to tailgate. No matter what the
weather was like, these fans would not miss a game. That's
how devoted WVU fans are and there aren't too many other
universities that could say the same about their school or
their fans. The fans' passion and dedication to our team is
something I've always appreciated, and as an athlete, it's
something you learn not to take for granted. Sometimes it's
the simple comfort of knowing the folks in the stands are in

your corner. That gives you the extra push you need to win the game.

Through their love and support, West Virginia University football had become a top program with some of the best athletes. While I was attending WVU, it seemed as if my fan base suddenly swelled and I gained many more followers. I found it pretty impressive that strangers were able to recite my background information without hesitation. Many fans knew more about me than some of my closest friends and that made me feel special.

During my high school football years, it was nice to look up into the bleachers and watch a crowd of 10,000 people cheering the team on. However, that was no comparison to my college football experience. Not only does WVU's football stadium seat over 60,000 fans, but people would also want to have their picture taken with me, ask me for my autograph and even want me to sign all sorts of things such as footballs, shirts and, on some occasions, body parts.

I remember during my senior season after my final game at Milan Puskar Stadium when I ran my last lap around the field; I went up into the stands to see fans that were so ecstatic over the win against our rival Pitt. One particular fan (who had followed my athletic journey since the day I stepped on campus) thought I was coming just to see her and was so excited to see me that she ran, fell down the steps, and ultimately injured her arm. She was ok, but that is definitely a moment that I would always remember. WVU's fans have truly made me feel like an A-list celebrity every single week and I'll never forget how loyal and dedicated they are.

To reward our faithful fans, we would have a few events to thank them for their dedicated support every year. Whether it was a special pep rally, or a "fan day," we could observe that they were very happy to have the football players and coaching staff recognize how grateful we were to see them go above and beyond to support our football team every week. I'm not sure if fans realize the impact that they have on our lives, but I'm as excited to see them support me, as they are excited to meet me. I have always made a point to acknowledge how appreciative I am for the commitment that the fans, my family and friends have showed me. I believe that it's very important to remember the people who have supported you on any challenging journey you made. Encouragement and kindness is not always a guarantee, so it's nice to give back to those who have been such a positive force of motivation for you.

Another reason why I chose to attend WVU was because of the team support that I felt when I visited the campus before committing to the school. At that time, as an outsider looking in, I could see that the players connected both on and off the field, and that was important to me. Even before I signed to attend WVU, I felt a sense of closeness to the coaches. We were able to communicate really well, which was essential to me since that's what I was used to. I had great relationships with my high school coaches and I wanted that to continue at the next level.

In college you realize that the people around you are those that you depend on. I could always count on the rest of the football team to support me in every aspect.

I remember another time during my senior season when my grandmother passed away at the beginning of training camp. Just about everyone including my coaches, fans, and teammates were very supportive during this tough time in my life. The coaches understood that I had to take time away to go home and miss crucial practices without any problems. The local WVU newspapers included her passing in their news, which soon created an appreciated outpouring of condolences to me from caring fans. So many players sent me texts, calls, etc. to show their support. We were much more than teammates, we were more like family. These are the men that I spent my Sunday dinners and holidays with instead of my parents since I was away from home. There are many teammates that I bonded with throughout my experience at WVU that remain in my life today. Through our seemingly endless drills and practices to the fun times we spent socializing, my football team from West Virginia University is one that I would never forget.

Another reason why I chose to join WVU was because of their academic program. There is a huge difference in the amount of school work that you receive in high school compared to college. Thankfully, I came prepared and was able to meet the challenge. However, knowing that WVU had a very structured program really helped me succeed, academically. I also credit some of my high school teachers and my parents for guiding me and giving me the discipline that I needed to study at the collegiate level.

Because I was on a full scholarship, I had the opportunity to take advantage of West Virginia University's study program for athletes. This included private tutors who were always available if we needed them. The tutors specialized in areas such as accounting, mathematics, or any other classes that troubled players. As a freshman, study hall was required on a daily basis. This type of structure helped to keep me focused on my grades and not on the parties.

Coaches were diligent in making sure that we attended study hall and always reminded us that we were "students first, and football players second." While many players did not want to hear this, to me, it made perfect sense. The coaches were very devoted to us staying on the right track. They not only wanted us to excel on the field, but also in our classes.

I watched too many people blow their college experience because of too much partying. As for me, I was ready to work day and night to get a good education, and prepare myself to be a key contributor on the football field. I always try to encourage young athletes to find a healthy balance between work and play. A student athlete's first priority and responsibility is to excel academically. An education is something no one can take away from you, no matter how the chips may fall when it comes to a professional career in sports. Practicing self-discipline and control off the field is a guaranteed way to help you practice it on the field; the two go hand in hand.

Our football team at West Virginia University was filled with players from all backgrounds. Some players would party too much, and before they knew it, they were off the team. Other players quit because they felt they were not getting enough playing time on the field, but you find that on pretty much every college level football team. Even I thought about transferring schools, because I was disappointed by how rarely we threw the football. However, I was in it for the long haul and could not separate myself from the WVU fans and my teammates.

Because of my dedication, hard work and discipline to my school work, I was able to graduate in three and a half years. These days, it's not unusual to find some students who take four and a half to five years before they are able to graduate. The pressures and stress of being a student athlete take a toll on many individuals, but my commitment to the game and to school continuously pushed me to stay focused.

Through thick and thin, through good weather and bad, through injuries and days that you wish never took place, I never lost my dedication to the game. To me, football was, and always will be, more than just a sport. It was an opportunity to show the world just how far I had come. It was a chance for me to practice and play hard, and to always do my best, no matter what obstacles suddenly jumped onto my path.

I always dreamed of playing professional football, and even during my high school football days, I had my doubts that it would ever happen. However, once I became a college football player, the dream seemed as if it just might come true. I believe that training makes the difference between success and failure. I had set my goals early in college to play professional football in the future, so it did not matter how difficult the training sessions were, I was on a mission to be a success.

Playing football can be a dangerous sport. Even in high school, many athletes suffered serious injuries, and unfortunately, a few football careers were cut short. I made it through my high school football years with only a few bumps and bruises, and even made it through my college football year as a freshman without a scratch.

However, right before the football season started during my sophomore year, I was not so lucky. I sustained a knee injury, and it was bad enough to keep me on the sideline for a few weeks; I had torn my meniscus in my left knee and had to have surgery. I was expecting to be in more pain than I was feeling, and was glad that it was not too intense. Thankfully, I have a high tolerance for pain, so I was able to get back in the game after only sitting out a few weeks. By mid-season I was back in the starting line-up. However, once the really cold weather arrived, my knee was giving me some more problems. That was a rough time, and it put a damper on my season. I was disappointed, but I did not let that hinder my ultimate goal: to play in the NFL.

The following year leading up to the start of the 2008-2009 football season, I injured the other knee with the same exact injury. According to the surgeon, in most cases when one knee meniscus is torn, the other will tear because of having to compensate more for the injured knee. Such a serious diagnosis might be discouraging to some, but I never lost hope and sight of getting back in the game as quickly as humanly possible. Once again, I had to overcome another obstacle, but my faith was able to help me stay positive, motivated and focused.

Leading up to my senior season I was coming off a great spring ball performance. I was rated as a top player in the NCAA by ESPN and had a 3rd to 5th round draft grade. I was very excited about the success I was having, until the first game of my senior season, when I was haunted by another injury. I was going out for a pass and the ball was thrown in the dirt. I reached down and made a shoe string catch, which led to me pulling my hamstring. Now I was out of the game once again, and hoped for another record breaking healing session. I managed to bounce back and continued to contribute the rest of the season.

West Virginia University has taught me a lot about myself as a person, student, and football player. I feel that I made the best decision by choosing to attend this university. The experience was not always pretty or pleasant, but it was real and I learned many lifelong lessons that attribute to my character today. The emotional and physical roller-coaster that my injuries caused taught me the importance of perseverance. Tough times don't last, but tough people do. If you can push through the pain and setbacks that life will undoubtedly bring you, progress and triumph is very often waiting for you. I established friendships and have many fans that I wouldn't trade for anything. These challenges and successes, friendly faces, and life lessons are what I will always remember about attending WVU.

WVU uses all-around effort to beat Pirates

By Dan Stefano
Associate Sports Editor

Head coach Rich Rodriguez of the No. 5 West Virginia University football team has seen plenty of impressive victories by his program over the past six-plus seasons.

But he called Saturday's 48-7 beat-down of East Carolina University the best overall performance his team has had in several years.

"I was very pleased with the way we played today in all three phases. I think we executed schemes well against a pretty good football team," Rodriguez said after the game.

And there was a lot to like about the win.

Mountaineer quarterback Patrick White bounced back from a so-so performance the week before at Maryland, as he went 18-for-20 through the air with two touchdowns. He also ran in two more scores.

Running back Steve Slaton ran 18 times for 110 yards and a touchdown, against a team that held him out of the end zone last season. The score gave him 42 touchdowns for his career, tying a school record shared by Ira Errett Rodgers and

See **East Carolina** page 2

West Virginia University receiver Wes Lyons blocks East Carolina's Leon Best into the ground, allowing fellow receiver Brandson Hogan to spring for a 9-yard gain in Saturday's game

69

SATURDAY, OCT. 11, 2008 WEST VIRGINIA VS. SYRACUSE GOALPOST THE DOMINION POST 17

A healthy Lyons hopes to build on momentum

STEFANIE LOH

Last weekend marked an auspicious beginning for Wes Lyons.

In his first collegiate start, the junior receiver from North Braddock, Pa. surpassed his 2006 yardage total, pulling in four catches for 47 yards.

Not bad for a guy coming back from an injury.

In his three years at WVU, Lyons has injured, and had surgery on, both knees. He had his right knee operated on last year, and he injured his left knee during fall camp this year and had to have it scoped.

Afterward, the recovery process took several weeks as Lyons worked to strengthen the knee and inch his way back to full health.

"After the first couple of games, I started to feel a little better," Lyons said. "I wouldn't say I'm 100 percent but I'm there, I'm just gonna continue to work at it."

He's had to work at a couple of other things over the years.

Showing emotion on the field isn't something that comes naturally to Lyons. He's a chill kind of guy.

At 6-foot-8, 226 pounds, he's tall, gangly, laid back and kind of quiet.

As wide receivers coach Lonnie Galloway puts it, "He's not somebody who's hooping and hollerin', not a rah-rah guy."

But even Galloway took a while to get used to Lyons' reserved countenance.

When he first sized up his receivers, Galloway said he tried to get Lyons to play with more passion.

In time, the coach realized that relaxed exterior aside, Lyons is not altogether devoid of fire and energy.

"In his own way, he does play with passion," Galloway said.

Galloway urged Lyons to inject that passion into all aspects of his game.

"It's not so much just (about) wanting the ball. Obviously they all want the football," Galloway said. "But just going out there, and blocking if it's blocking that we need, just getting the mentality of 'I gotta do this, got to get down there.' Anything. Just making plays."

"Just showing the passion, which, the last couple of weeks, he's done."

Lyons is hoping to do a lot more. He spent the offseason working on his technique, especially his blocking technique.

"I've spent a lot of time on blocking, especially the last couple of years," Lyons said.

Like the rest of the team, he also went

SEE **LYONS**, 18

STEFANIE LOH is a sports reporter for The Dominion Post. Write to her at sloh@dominionpost.com.

West Virginia receiver **Wes Lyons** has had to battle nagging knee injuries the last two seasons. The 6-foot-8 receiver is close to being healthy and is showing it. He caught four passes for 44 yards in last week's victory against Rutgers.

Brown gets QB down

Looks sharp in situational passing drills

WVU FOOTBALL NOTEBOOK

BY STEFANIE LOH
The Dominion Post

After being completely overwhelmed by their own defense Friday, the WVU Mountaineers' first-team offense showed up ready to play Saturday morning.

For the first time this spring, the football team donned full pads and lined up for full-contact situational scrimmages.

The passing game flourished under the direction of quarterback Jarrett Brown, who went 11-for-11 for more than 110 yards in the final two offensive skeleton (offense vs. defense but with no linemen) sequences.

"These first three days he's been really sharp, and that's a tribute to Jarrett," offensive coordinator Jeff Mullen said. "He now understands, this is his time. We've talked about that a lot in the offseason, and in the last three months he's put in a lot of time. He's about done with his schoolwork now."

But there's a tremendous gulf between Brown and the rest of the Mountaineers' quarterbacks.

Coley White, the only other scholarship quarterback on the roster this spring, took all the second-team reps but struggled to complete medium- and long-range passes. With no other signal-callers to go to, walk-ons Josh DePasquale and Ian Loy are helping to throw passes to the receivers in drills.

This resulted in several poorly thrown passes and missed connections when the receivers went one-on-one against the defensive backs Saturday morning.

"Depth is always a concern and clearly it's most evident at the quarterback position because you can see the ball float," said Mullen, who

is also the quarterbacks coach. "These poor kids have no idea what they're doing. So if we can at least get Coley going in the right direction, we'll continue to work with Coley."

Solid in the slot

With Jock Sanders still suspended for a DUI arrest in March, senior Carmen Connolly has taken over at slot receiver, and he's making the most of his opportunity.

Connolly caught passes of 21 and 14 yards during the offensive pass skeleton, and also looked nimble during the "Victory" drill the team opened practice with.

In the victory drill, the ball carrier has to run through a gauntlet of three defenders.

"When you lose a player of [Sanders'] caliber, it's a huge blow, so I'm just trying to do the best I can, and I'm taking a couple of extra reps since he's not here," Connolly said. "Jarrett [Brown] is doing a terrific job coming in and taking a leadership role on the team, so that also makes it easier."

SEE **NOTEBOOK**, 5-C

WES 'BIG TREE' LYONS plants himself in the end zone and catches five TD passes Saturday. **Page 3-C.**

Draft Prep

CHAPTER SEVEN

"Do not go where the path may lead; go instead where there is no path and leave a trail"
- Ralph Waldo Emerson

It was official. I was now a graduate of West Virginia University and my senior season was over. It was time for me to leave Morgantown, WV. That was a sad day because I didn't know if I would ever see these players and classmates again, but I knew that I was moving on to bigger and better things. The NFL was all I could think about after another disappointing college season. I knew that although the collegiate chapter of my life was over, the sky was the limit for the next phase of my life and I was excited.

The first step that I needed to take in his journey was to pick an NFL agent to represent me. This was a hard process, because there had been numerous agents contacting me through several different sources. I would get calls at home, emails, and even Facebook messages. The experience was reminiscent of my college recruitment and I was reminded of how important this decision would be. I could not be signed with an agent until my senior season was over, so this didn't leave a lot of time to evaluate all of my options and make a decision. I was at the point where I needed to get down to business and pick the best one for me. I screened some of them to determine how they became an agent, who their former and current clients were, etc. I went out to dinner with other agents and talked in great detail about my plans, hopes and dreams. It was important that I selected an agent that was on the same page as me. I really needed to connect with that person and feel that he truly had my best interest at heart.

Finally, my decision would be made from one of two agents, either Robert or Joe. Joe was in contact with my father more than he was with me, and it was hard to reach him sometimes. Robert, on the other hand, reached out to me and seemed to be more interested. I felt that I needed someone with whom I could communicate easily with; so I picked Robert. He had a great plan for me and I thought it was the best option for me at the time.

Robert arranged for my training to take place in North Carolina and I felt as if I was living the life. He also arranged a condo for me to live in, along with paying me weekly stipends. Not only did Robert take care of providing food for the condo, but he also took me out to eat several times a week. Besides all of the perks, there were grueling training sessions. I lifted weights, ran sprints, and worked on drills with former NFL wide receivers five days a week. On the weekends, I attended a yoga class to help strengthen my core. At first I was intimated by the other players who were there, but when I realized I was just as qualified as they were, it made a big difference in how I would handle and endure the daily practices and workout sessions. At that point, I realized just how important having confidence would be if I was going to continue and have a career as a professional football player. All of this work was to prepare myself and other athletes for the NFL combine (an invitation-only workout).

Unfortunately, I was not invited to the NFL combine, but I had another opportunity at West Virginia's pro-day to impress NFL scouts. After three months of training, I felt I was beyond ready to showcase my ability to the NFL scouts. Heading into pro-day, I was under the radar as a player coming into the draft. I would be sure to make that change after pro-day. After having a not-so-great senior season, I needed a strong pro-day to even get a look from the NFL.

A few days before pro-day, all of the former athletes were coming into Morgantown, WV to get ready to perform. My agent flew me in a day before and paid for a hotel for me to stay in. The day I got into Morgantown, I received a call from a Pittsburgh Steelers scout. He said that the Steelers organization would like to have a meeting with me an hour before pro-day started. I was excited to learn that my hometown team was interested in me. The scout I met with said that they were going to keep a close eye on me as I performed that day. I had butterflies as I left our meeting and headed to get ready to showcase my ability, but I knew that I had a job to do. The butterflies went away after seeing my agent and father, along with other friends who were there to support me. I was ready to exceed the expectations everyone had for me. I had trained my entire life for this moment and I was going to prove that I belonged in the NFL.

Pro-day consisted of running a 40 yard dash, vertical jump, broad jump, 225 pound bench press max and position drills. The only thing I was nervous about was running my

40 yard dash because I was inconsistent in my time. While I was in North Carolina, I would run between a low 4.5 to a mid-4.6 so I was hoping for the best. I was very confident in everything else and it showed.

The day started off by doing several different measurements such as height, weight, length of hand, and length of your arms. I was six feet eight inches tall and I weighed 235 pounds. After the weigh-in, we got ready for the vertical jump. I knocked all of the markers off with my first jump. After I gave the scouts time to raise the bar, I proceeded, jumped and knocked down every marker except three. I was measured to have a 41.5 inch vertical jump. This was unheard of for a guy who is 6'8", unless his name is LeBron James. Over thirty scouts were there and they all looked astonished.

The rest of the pro-day went well. I benched 225 pounds 18 times, and I ran a 4.6 in the 40 yard dash. I was disappointed about the 40 yard dash, but I was having such a good day otherwise and needed to finish strong. The final part of pro-day was the position drills, which I knew I would excel in. Jarrett Brown (former WVU quarterback) was throwing to me and Alric Arnett (former WVU wide receiver). I caught every pass thrown my way and even stretched my 6'8" frame out to make a few spectacular catches. As I finished my workout, scouts came to speak to me and my agent. They said that I made some money with my performance. Hearing that made my day, but knowing that my father thought I looked great, meant so much more! I felt that I had his approval, which was far more important to me than any NFL scout or coach. Once again, my hard work and self-discipline had paid off. The grueling training sessions, strict schedules, and sacrifice had helped me to deliver in a very crucial moment. I was excited and could not wait to see what the future held.

With pro-day being in March, the draft was still an entire month away. I had a lot of waiting to do, but I was hoping to see my name called on draft day. I spent most of this time with my family and two friends, Kirk and Jalloh, who kept me busy working out. Leading up to the draft, I received calls on my personal cell phone from six different teams. They were saying that they were looking to draft me, but possibly in the late rounds. They would ask for other family member's phone numbers in case my number was busy as they tried to reach me.

My agent would reach out to teams as well, but he seemed to be getting some backlash against me. The backlash that he was hearing came from the West Virginia University coaches and staff. They were saying negative things about all of the players who were entering the NFL draft that year. I've heard about this happening to former players at WVU leading up to the draft, but I never thought it would happen to me since I was very respectful to everyone. The NFL is hard enough to get into, and I did not need anything extra holding me back. You would think that the WVU staff would want their athletes in the NFL to make the university look better. However, that was not the case for these coaches. As you see, very few athletes from WVU get drafted or they fall further down in the draft than expected. Thankfully, West Virginia recently had a clean sweep by hiring new coaches and staff who are more concerned about helping their players get to the next level rather than holding athletes back.

Although there was some negative feedback, I still believed that I had a chance to be drafted because I had received calls from several different teams during the week of the draft. I watched the draft with just a few family members, anxiously waiting for my cell phone to ring. We continued watching as each draft round unfolded and it got intense around the sixth round, as I kept looking at my phone. Next thing you know, it was the seventh round, and I still did not receive a phone call. As the draft was finished, I waited for a call to be signed as a free agent... still no call. I was puzzled, so I called my agent and asked him about it. He said not to worry because this situation happened often: you might not get a call on the first day, but within a few days, he was very confident that the right call would come through. I tried my best to stay positive, and I tried not to worry. Many of my friends were getting picked up, and they kept telling me, "Wes, man, you should have been picked up by now!" It was a long, drawn out waiting period, that's for sure. I was very disappointed that I wasn't drafted, but I was still hoping that things would work out for me.

Adversity Strikes

CHAPTER EIGHT

"We are pressed on every side by troubles, but we are not crushed. We are perplexed, but not driven to despair. We are hunted down, but never abandoned by God. We get knocked down, but we are not destroyed."
- 2 Corinthians 4:8-9

The draft was over and I had not been drafted. This was a tough time for me, emotionally and mentally. I had media from West Virginia calling to see which NFL team I signed with, but I hadn't been signed. I would ignore all phone calls as I waited in disappointment with dwindling hope. Finally, two days after the draft I received a call from the New York Jets. This was still not the call I was hoping for, but they said they would bring me in for their minicamp. I was beyond shocked that nobody was willing to sign me after all the calls I received leading up to the draft. This was going to be an uphill battle. I had to go into this minicamp and take one of the veteran player's spots within three days, to earn a NFL contract. This seemed impossible, but I kept a positive mind and set forth to do just that.

As I started my journey to become a New York Jet, I met another guy named Mick Williams at the airport. Mick had signed a contract with the NY Jets and we would be taking this journey together. He was a University of Pittsburgh graduate and played at the defensive end position. Being rivals in college gave us something to talk about on the plane ride. As we were up in the air, the very small plane began to shake, going up and down with turbulence. At times the plane would drop about five feet and then the pilot would regain control. Everyone on the plane who was asleep was now startled awake. Mick, who was next to me, along with other people on the plane, began to experience nausea. The turbulence continued the remaining hour of the trip. By the time we landed, several people were sick. This was a rough beginning to my NFL experience and I nervously wondered if it was a foreshadowing of what was to come.

By the time we got to New York, neither Mick nor I felt well. We were picked up by New York Jets employees and went to take care of the medical side of football, which entailed filling out paper work and getting physicals. After that was finished, we met the coaches and got our playbooks. As soon as I got that playbook I began to study, since I was a student of the game. The self-discipline I had developed in college would be more important than ever, if I was going to make the most of this opportunity. The next few days were going to be long and demanding. My schedule included two practices for the next two days and then one practice on the final day before I went home.

I wasn't asked to do much during my first practice because the coaches felt that I didn't know the offense since I was just given the playbook the night before. Little did they know, I had studied late into the night and taken notes in the meetings we had before practice, so I knew a good portion of the playbook. Later that day during the second practice I got a lot of reps. I made some nice plays that got me noticed by the veteran players and the coaches. Over the next couple of days, I made catches over players and won battles against their number one draft pick, Kyle Wilson. Once minicamp was over, I was hoping to be signed since I was having a meeting with head coach Rex Ryan. To my dismay, he told me he would recommend me to any team, but another wide receiver was something they did not need at the time.

I feared this situation may happen, but it did not keep me from pursuing my goal. Pushing my disappointment aside, I relied more heavily on my faith and focused on keeping my body and mind prepared for my next opportunity.

During this time, I moved to Ohio with my brother so I could focus and not be distracted by family and friends back home in Pittsburgh. One of the most difficult things I faced was explaining to everyone what happened with the New York Jets. So to prevent those questions from being asked, I went away. I was staying in Akron, Ohio and I worked out at The University of Akron. The football staff enjoyed me being around and let me use all of their facilities. I also helped out their players by teaching them different techniques and other skills that I learned with the New York Jets. Working out with these guys helped me keep my mind clear.

It was tough to stay focused, especially because my father was becoming ill. He was suffering from a heart virus and his health had become a major concern. I would travel from Akron to Pittsburgh on the weekends to check on both of my parents. My father was trying to get me to move back to Pittsburgh to work out with my old track coach, Mathis "Boo" Harrison. But I just did not want to be bothered by anyone, so I continued to stay in Akron.

Sometimes I would have negative thoughts as I waited for another opportunity to come around. I wondered if I would ever sign a NFL contract. The time alone with my thoughts created dangerous territory to slip into a state of discouragement.

My spirits were lifted when I heard from the Pittsburgh Steelers. One of the Steelers scouts said they would see how camp went and sign me to their roster if a wide receiver was injured. With renewed hope, I even drove to Latrobe, Pennsylvania, where the Steelers' camp was located, to meet with the scout who was interested in me. However, this turned out to be another disappointment. The Steelers were starting their season and no one was injured for me to take their place.

I continued to stay in Akron until my father was checked into the hospital. He was having heart trouble and the doctors scheduled him to have open heart surgery. I worked out while I was in Pittsburgh and stayed in town until he was supposed to have surgery. After learning that his surgery was pushed back a few weeks, I decided to return to Akron. For some reason, I could not stop training. I just wanted to get back to a NFL team. Focusing on my goal was a much needed distraction from the stress my father's health issues were causing. There was nothing our family could do to help except stay prayerful and hope for the best. It was more important at the time to be getting stronger and faster, than to be in a hospital for most of my day. In my mind, football was the most important priority. Even when my father was set to have the surgery, I did not believe it was as serious as he made it seem. My father was known to exaggerate often (whether jokingly or to further dramatize a serious situation), and that tendency made me believe he was exaggerating the seriousness of his upcoming surgery.

I came home the night before my father was scheduled to have his surgery. He told me I would be great in the NFL and he was proud of everything I had accomplished. I stayed only a short period of time, so he could get some rest for his surgery. I wished him good luck as we parted ways. I checked on him the next day and the doctor said it would be a week before he would awake from the surgery.

So, I drove back to Akron and continued to train. My brother and I would call daily to check on our father and we visited on the weekend. The doctor pushed back the time to wake my father and I began to suspect that something was wrong. I planned to come home and get some answers. The day before I was planning to come home, the doctor called my brother and me. I could tell by his voice that something was wrong. The doctor said my father wasn't going to make it through the night. I was in total shock! My brother and I headed to the hospital immediately. I prayed the entire way to the hospital, as my brother informed some family members to meet us there.

Once we all arrived at the hospital, the doctors said our father definitely wasn't going to make it. I held my father's right hand and my brother held his left hand, as our dad passed away. I was crushed. I had lost my number one fan and the only person I ever depended on.

There was not much time to be sad since there was so much work to do. My brother and I were all my father had. We put together the funeral arrangements, and moved his things out of his apartment within a day. It was amazing the things my brother and I could do together. It was very much because of the sense of teamwork and cooperation my father instilled in us that we were able to work together through such a difficult situation. I took two weeks off from working out to navigate through that tragic time. Then with a revived sense of determination, I set out to honor my father and began to train again. This increased my drive and focus to another level. I was going to get to the NFL no matter what.

Failure Is Not an Option

CHAPTER NINE

"Commit your actions to the Lord, and your plans will

succeed"

-Proverbs 16:3

Losing a loved one is never easy, but it is always best to

keep their memory alive in your heart by honoring their

legacy. I realized that I had to get back into a regular

workout and training routine, which also helped me to move

forward in my life. In this case, my father always believed

in me, and before his passing he reaffirmed that I was a

great football player. So to honor his legacy, I continued to

work hard.

Before I knew it, the Steelers were asking me to

come to Pittsburgh for a workout. It was a great experience,

and I gave it everything I had. This workout did not involve

a lot of activity. They only asked me to run a few routes, and gave me a physical and took x-rays. The route that I ran the most was a fade route going into the end zone. This was an area that the Steelers were hoping to improve on. I ran ten fade routes in a row and made some spectacular catches. The scouts who were there were all very impressed. They requested to have a meeting that followed the workout. In this meeting, the scouts said to stay ready and that they might sign me as they were going into their playoff run. It felt great to finally see a possible opportunity.

Not too long afterwards, I was asked to go to another workout. This time it was with the Cincinnati Bengals. The Bengal's head coach, Marvin Lewis, had been a longtime family friend and he decided to give me an opportunity to work out for his team. I was excited for the chance and was prepared to do my best. When I arrived, I saw that their conditions were not the most ideal for the workout. It was the middle of January and there was no indoor facility. This meant that I had to do the workout outside in the snow. Although this was not the best climate, I managed to do well.

The Bengals season had been over and they decided to sign another wide receiver. Now my only hope was for the Steelers to sign me. They were headed to the Super

Bowl and unfortunately did not sign me throughout the playoffs. The Steelers decided they would sign me, but not until after the NFL lockout was over. My experiences at the professional level were teaching me that nothing in the NFL was promised, so I had to take it upon myself to go above and beyond to show that I deserved an opportunity to play. While the Steelers were away for the Super Bowl, I played in a flag football game in Cleveland, OH. During this particular game, my brother recorded some of the plays on his cell phone. In one play that he captured, I jumped over another player and caught the ball.

I was able to upload the video footage of my spectacular jump and catch, along with footage of myself bench pressing 225 pounds to get attention from NFL teams. I also had my agent send the video directly to the Steelers to review. After returning home from a tough Super Bowl loss, the Steelers signed me the next day. This was the best feeling in my life. Finally, I signed that NFL contract that I longed for. The scout who called me even mentioned the catch that I made from the video when he asked me to join the team. Thank goodness I had taken action to get noticed and make it happen. This experience taught me to not wait for an opportunity to happen. It is best to take things into your own hands and create one. If you want something bad enough in life, you will work hard and go above and beyond the call of duty to make it happen!

After the Super Bowl, most players take time off to relax and enjoy themselves, but I did not. I used that time to continue training and met with the coaches since I was new to the team. I read the playbook and memorized everything I could. In short, I kept myself busy and kept moving forward in my football career. Unfortunately, I could only meet with coaches and train at the Steelers facility for a short period of time due to the NFL lockout. During the lockout, players were unable to contact coaches or use the facility.

With the lockout in full effect, I started to work out with a small group of NFL athletes from different teams. Terence Johnson (Colts), Darrin Walls (Falcons), Brennan Marion (Dolphins), Ryan Mundy (Steelers), and Tyler Grisham (Steelers). We met up with my old track coach, Mathis "Boo" Harrison, who trained us. Our workouts were at a high intensity level. We had seven NFL players pushing each other every day, as we prepared for camp. I recall a time when Ryan and I were competing the entire workout, whether it was in drills or during sprints. We counted and kept track of each sprint we won. We even raced on the cool down lap after our crucial workout session. The other five players would watch as the competition was getting fierce. The result of the competition was a draw, but if he were to tell the story, he would say he won. Of course, I would say I did. I loved days like that one, when we competed, because it made us all better. All athletes have pride and love to win, but competing gave us that extra push to do more.

This small group of athletes that I worked out with helped me to stay competitive and improve on my skills to succeed professionally. I make it a point in my life to continuously surround myself with positive and productive people. I believe in the saying, "you are who you surround yourself with." Even though there was a lockout in place, I knew it was important to find ways to progress. It would have been easy to do the bare minimum since I was not required to practice, but I used this as an opportunity to get better.

As the NFL lockout went longer than expected, Ben Roethlisberger personally reached out to all of the offensive players and scheduled a time for us to meet at a local high school. We would run plays and do drills. These practices were scheduled to help keep football on the minds of some of the players. As for me, football was all I thought about. I would work out with my trainer, and then go work out with my new team. These workout sessions with Ben gave me a good grasp of the offense, since it was new to me. I would run plays and if I was watching, I would take mental notes. I knew that I would be more than ready mentally and physically heading into camp.

The lockout was finally lifted and NFL camps were set to begin. I was thrilled with excitement to prove to everyone that I could play on a NFL field. I had trained and studied hard all year leading up to camp. As camp began, I made one of the best plays in camp on the second day of practice. I jumped over two defenders going across the middle of the field. This play along with others gained me a lot of attention from the coaches. Through my performance in camp, I began to earn the players and coaches' respect as a NFL wide receiver. Now, all they wanted to see was my performance in a game.

We had four preseason games. Throughout three weeks of practice leading up to the first preseason game, I earned playing time with the second team. The second play of my first NFL game I was injured with a concussion. This caused me to be sidelined for the rest of the game. The following week I made my first NFL catch, along with another catch for a touchdown, which was called back due to a misalignment by another player. My coach was excited for me, and called me on the sideline from the booth to express how well I was doing. I managed to do well in the last two games, earning catches in each. In those four games, I was third for receiving yards on the team. These statistics, along with other players providing a lot of positive feedback, led me to think that I was guaranteed a spot on the final roster.

The final cuts were the following day after the fourth preseason game. I was pretty confident that I had a spot. As I went to the Steelers facility to get treatment on my knee that I injured the day before, I was called into the coach's office. To my astonishment, he told me they were releasing me. Coach Tomlin also said that they might sign me back, but they only had a short time period to get down to 53 players. In that moment, I learned that sometimes situations are simply out of your control. I knew how hard I worked and how well I performed. I practiced and studied when other players were relaxing because playing football is what I loved to do. This experience reminded me that life is all about being resilient. Situations often occur that may cause disappointment and discouragement, but how you bounce back and overcome obstacles is what is important. No matter what the challenge is that you are faced with, it is essential to stay focused and be patient. I have had to overcome several adversities throughout my journey, but I never lost faith. Now after learning that I was released, the only thing that I could do was accept the decision the Steelers had made and continue to move forward.

First NFL catch

The League

CHAPTER TEN

"Everyone who competes in the games goes into strict training. They do it to get a crown that will not last; but we do it to get a crown that will last forever"
- 1 Corinthians 9:25

After being released, I was disappointed because I knew that I showcased an ability that surpassed other players. However, this was not the end for me. I held on to hope that I might be signed back and I maintained a positive attitude. Two days after I was released, the Steelers called and said they were making changes in an attempt to sign me back. Three weeks went by and I still had not heard from the team, so I returned to my old stomping grounds of Morgantown, West Virginia for training. It was good to be back there because not only did I get good training sessions from the strength coaches, but Alric Arnett and Jarrett Brown were there for me to workout with as well.

After about two weeks of training in Morgantown, I received a call from the Houston Texans. They wanted to bring me in for a workout because their injured wide receiver, Andre Johnson, was set to miss some time. As I was boarding the plane to Houston, I ran into some Steelers fans. They stated how displeased they were to see that I was released, and reassured me by expressing how well I performed during my time on the team. Seeing that other people noticed the hard work, that I devoted, gave me confidence going into my workout with the Texans.

When I showed up for the workout, there were all tight ends there. They were asking me to play a little at the tight end position. I did tight end drills and wide receiver drills. We also did a 225 rep max on the bench press and ran a 40 yard dash. I was the fastest and the second strongest guy there. As we did our drills, I was the best on the field by far, and some of these guys played in the NFL for several years. I ran better routes and caught everything thrown my way. I saw how pleased the coaches were with my performance.

Each player had a meeting with the coaches following the workout and I had high hopes because of how well I did. There were five coaches in the meeting room and they started the conversation saying, "We want to sign you today." Just hearing those words made me feel a burst of excitement, but I tried to hold my poker face and maintain a businesslike demeanor. As the conversation went on, I heard a "BUT." To make a long story short, they said they needed to sign a defensive back and would then sign me at the first opportunity they had.

I returned home to Pittsburgh hoping it wouldn't be long before I left to play as a Houston Texan. Waiting is something I began to get familiar with as I continued my training. Months went by and the season was drawing nearer to a close. I had also worked out with the Saint Louis Rams and was then looking to be signed at the end of the season. At that point, the Steelers said they were no longer interested in me, but fortunately, the Texans were still highly interested in me, and said that they would sign me after the season. Every team handles their off-season differently. Some teams sign players right after the season ends and others wait until the draft. The Texans were planning to sign me after the 2012 NFL draft. I felt myself being in a position similar to the one I was in before I signed with the Steelers. I knew that nothing was promised in the NFL so it was time for me to make something happen.

WVU was having their pro-day so I thought it would be a good opportunity to participate. I weighed myself in, did the bench press, and ran a 40 yard dash. I ran a faster time than I ran two years ago when I first came out of college. I also benched pressed 28 reps with 225 pounds, compared to 18 reps two years prior. Then I watched the rest of pro-day and saw how the other WVU athletes performed.

Mike Tomlin was in attendance and called my cell phone to come across the field to talk to him. He decided to sign me back right there on the spot. This was another example of me following my gut intuition. I knew it was time for me to make something happen to get what I wanted, and my instincts were right. Coach Tomlin also wanted to sign Will Johnson, a player who went unnoticed the year before in the draft. We both were very excited, but Coach Tomlin through a curve ball at me, and said that he wanted me to play tight end.

This was an interesting situation that I was in. I had proven myself at the wide receiver position and made a connection with the wide receiver coach, but now I had a new coach who I felt did not like me for unknown reasons. The receiver's coach was still helping me as we went through our off-season workouts, while the tight end coach gave me no guidance. For me to be playing a position that I had no experience in, you would think that I would get a little help from the coach. The only two people who helped me learn the position over the next few months were Heath Miller and David Johnson (Pittsburgh Steelers Tight ends). They worked with me after practice and gave me tips when watching film. I began to get good at this new position and I started to make plays.

The final day of minicamp, I was coming off my best practice yet. We had one day left and then we were off for five weeks until training camp. The next morning, I was headed out dressed and ready to practice, until Coach Tomlin stopped me to say they were releasing me temporarily. There were a lot of other players hurt and they had to get through one day of practice. There were a certain number of players who could practice each day and the Steelers had just signed a veteran linebacker. Coach Tomlin told me face to face that he was going to sign me "right back" after they made a few changes in the five weeks period leading into training camp.

I was very understanding because over the last three years, I saw how the business worked. Players get cut almost on a daily basis, whether it's during the season or the off-season. I was confident I would be signed back because the coach gave me his word. I also had my room for camp set up and talked to a few veteran players on the team, who said the Steelers were usually good about their word. I left all my belongings in my locker, knowing that this was a short term situation. In the days that led up to camp, I continued to work out as I prepared for my return. I was on a mission to get bigger and stronger to play this new position to the best of my ability.

Over the five weeks period leading up to camp, I participated in Charlie Batch's youth basketball league by helping him in any way that he needed assistance. Working with the kids brightened each of my days and made me passionate about helping the youth. Growing up, I had many influential people who were devoted to helping me stay on the right path and be involved in the community. I embrace being a positive role model to young children now that I have the opportunity to be an encouraging influence.

As the starting date of camp came closer, the Steelers continued to say that they would sign me, but they never did. Mike Tomlin always referred to the NFL as "a grown man business." I had learned first-hand... it truly was. There would be lies told, unfair treatment, and unfortunate circumstances. Most people see the NFL as a game for grown men, but it's more of a business that makes decisions based on that concept.

Every player has his own path, but the best thing to do is to stay positive and continue to move forward. I have learned that it is important to always focus on your end goal. By doing this, you can overcome any challenge that arises in the process. Through training, preparation and dedication, you will be equipped to conquer anything to be successful. The Lord will open doors to provide the right opportunities and close doors that are not meant to be. Throughout my journey in the NFL, I met great people and I had amazing experiences. I will continue to make a path that is guided by the Lord. He has a plan for everyone and I believe everything happens for a reason. For every athlete, there will be tough times on and off the field. To succeed, you must be patient. It is important to have a dream — to protect it and fight for it. I encourage you to let patience be the thread that weaves that dream together. Dreams don't become reality overnight, but in one way or another they do come true. My journey is far from over, and the lessons I've learned thus far have given me the confidence to continue down the path God is guiding me to blaze.

"I focus on this one thing: Forgetting the past and looking forward to what lies ahead, I press on to reach the end of the race and receive the heavenly prize for which God, through Christ Jesus, is calling us."

- Philippians 3:13:14

Made in the USA
Charleston, SC
11 March 2013